THE

BIG
FEELINGS

SURVIVAL GUIDE

THIS BOOK BELONGS TO:

~~~~~~~~~~~~~~~~~~~~~~~~~

THE
BIG
FEELINGS
SURVIVAL GUIDE

A Creative Workbook for Mental Health

ALYSE RURIANI

ATR, LPC

WORKMAN PUBLISHING • NEW YORK

For you, for me, and for all the big, beautiful,
messy feelings we experience in life.

Library of Congress Cataloging-in-Publication Data is available.

ISBN 978-1-5235-1593-6

Design by Sarah Smith

Workman books are available at special discounts when purchased in bulk for premiums and sales promotions as well as for fundraising or educational use. Special editions or book excerpts can also be created to specification. For details, contact the Special Sales Director at specialmarkets@hbgusa.com.

Workman Publishing Co., Inc., a subsidiary of Hachette Book Group, Inc.
1290 Avenue of the Americas
New York, NY 10104

workman.com

WORKMAN is a registered trademark of Workman Publishing Co., Inc.,
a subsidiary of Hachette Book Group, Inc.

Printed in China on responsibly sourced paper.

First printing March 2023

10 9 8 7 6 5 4 3 2 1

Citations: page 2: Linehan, 2015; page 4: AATA, 2017; page 33: Ratson, 2017; page 59: Steiner, 2022; page 85: Firestone, 2015

CONTENTS

INTRODUCTION

I remember sitting in the self-help aisle of the bookstore as a teenager, flipping through book after book after book, looking for something that could help me. A lot of those books had information that was useful, but often the language used was so clinical and cold that I had a hard time connecting with it. I wanted something that would help, but also something that was engaging. I loved dialectical behavior therapy (DBT) and art therapy, two (very different) types of therapy I was receiving at the time. I dreamed of a book that combined them, but it seemed like there were only two options: books that were creative *or* books that were clinical. I found myself yearning for something that didn't seem to exist—a creative workbook that provided evidence-based skills and tips to help my mental health. Since it didn't exist, I told myself that when I got through this, I would make one.

Fast forward to now—I am an art therapist, counselor, graphic designer, and illustrator with lived experience of my own mental health struggles. I've both provided and utilized dialectical behavior therapy and art therapy, and I've even found ways to combine the two. I recognize the ways that skills from DBT and methods from art therapy can be useful outside the therapy room, too, and assist people in taking care of themselves and their mental health. Then I remembered that idea I had many years ago . . . and realized it was time.

Maybe you've also sat on the floor of the self-help section of the bookstore (or scrolled endlessly online) looking for something like this. Maybe you didn't know you were looking for something like this, but it found its way to you. Whatever the reason this book is now in your hands, I hope it provides the support you need. I hope you can take what you learn and create within these pages and apply it out in the world. I hope that you can experience the value that lies in dedicating time to your well-being, connecting with your creativity, and learning practical skills we can all use each day to engage in self-care, cope with life, and take care of our mental health.

About This Book

This workbook combines the concepts and skills from a therapy called dialectical behavior therapy (DBT) with a creative approach influenced by art therapy.

What Is Dialectical Behavior Therapy?

Dialectical behavior therapy is a revolutionary, evidence-based treatment approach created by Marsha Linehan, PhD. It was developed to treat people dealing with chronic suicidality and borderline personality disorder but has since been applied in a wide variety of uses, clinical and nonclinical alike. Traditional DBT treatment includes a skills training group, individual DBT therapy, phone coaching, and a consultation group for the therapists. Today, DBT skill training has expanded and shown to be effective well outside of the traditional framework. What does that mean? Simply put, it means that DBT skills can be beneficial for anyone!

One of the core concepts in DBT is right in the title: dialectics. "Dialectics" are two seemingly opposite things can both be true at the same time. The main dialectic within DBT (and honestly, in therapy in general) is that of acceptance *and* change. That we can accept ourselves while also changing our actions, emotions, and thoughts. These skills are not mutually exclusive, and we are more effective at reaching our goals when we can hold both.

DBT consists of four modules that address different aspects of emotional and mental well-being; each module contains practical skills.

MINDFULNESS

This is the cornerstone of DBT, in that many mindfulness concepts and skills are used in the other modules. Mindfulness is about being present in the moment, by focusing our attention on the here and now. Mindfulness skills help us to be aware of what is going on within ourselves and the world around us, which in turn helps us to slow down and proceed more effectively.

DISTRESS TOLERANCE

Distress tolerance is about getting through moments of intense emotions. We use distress tolerance skills when our emotions have overwhelmed our ability to cope and we are in need of short-term skills to survive the current distressing moment.

EMOTIONAL REGULATION

Emotional regulation is about identifying, understanding, adjusting, and managing our emotions. The skills in this section help us to have a better grasp on the purpose of emotions and learn ways to cope with uncomfortable feelings.

INTERPERSONAL EFFECTIVENESS

Interpersonal effectiveness is about navigating relationships. The skills in this section help us to communicate with others, manage conflict, and create and maintain healthy relationships.

What Is Art Therapy?

It can be difficult to describe art therapy because it exists in so many forms and is used in so many ways for so many different reasons. In this type of therapy, a trained art therapist employs creative processes and art-making with their clients to address clients' goals. The process of making art and the artwork itself can give people new ways to express themselves, access and identify emotions, connect with their bodies, explore difficult experiences, and communicate with others.

Art therapy is used in clinical settings (such as hospitals or outpatient therapy centers) as well as nonclinical settings (such as community centers or schools). Regardless of the type of setting, art therapy is facilitated by an art therapist—someone who receives specific training and education on art therapy and psychotherapy.

Creativity and art-making in general can be beneficial tools for our mental health. Many people already utilize art as a coping skill, tool for growth, and avenue for healing outside of formal art therapy. The benefits of art and art therapy are not exclusive to those who identify as artists or creatives—you don't have to be "good" at art (whatever that means) in order to benefit from art therapy or therapeutic art-making! So, if you were reading this and thinking, "That's not for me . . . I can't draw," I'm here to tell you, "Art therapy is for everyone, and, yes, you *can*!"

Navigating This Book

The book is split into four chapter sections: WTF (What's the Feeling?); Anger; Fear; and Sadness. You can think of WTF as the "home base" of the book—it has prompts to help you identify and understand what emotion(s) you are feeling. Once you determine what emotion you are experiencing, you can identify its "parent" emotion: anger, fear, or sadness. Head to the chapter dedicated to that emotion, pick a prompt (any prompt) from within the section, and do it! Repeat as necessary. Of course, you might already know what emotion you're experiencing. If that's the case, feel free to turn to the appropriate chapter and start with any exercise that feels right to you!

Each prompt throughout the book is based on a skill from one of the four DBT modules or from art therapy. There will be a little icon and label at the bottom of each page to identify which DBT module is being used. This information provides context for where the skill is coming from and helps you understand how the work you are doing relates back to DBT. As you use this book and take note of the icons, you might begin noticing how skills from different modules help in different ways. You might even start identifying what module would be most helpful to you in any given moment, and intentionally seek out those prompts.

MINDFULNESS

DISTRESS TOLERANCE

EMOTIONAL REGULATION

INTERPERSONAL EFFECTIVENESS

ART THERAPY

On some pages, you will see a note under the skill name that reads "Part of the _____ skills" (see page 12 for the first instance). This means that the DBT skill on that page is part of a larger set of skills that relate to one another and are often used together. Turn to the Skill Sets appendix on page 114 to learn more about these.

Now, if you're like me, you might still have questions like:

To these questions I say, don't worry, I got you. If you're not sure what emotion you're feeling even after using a WTF prompt, that's okay! Pick any section. If you're feeling more than one emotion, that's okay, too. Welcome to being human! Choose one emotion to work on first, then you can do another. How you choose a prompt from within a chapter is up to you. Here are some ideas:

- Go in chronological order.

- Open to a random page.

- Flip through and pick the prompt that you think you need right now.

- Use dice! There are 17 to 20 prompts in each section, so you can even use a 20-sided die.

- Use a random number-generator online—you can input the page range and let it select a page for you.

- Use your intuition; close your eyes and flip through the pages until you feel called to stop.

- Phone a friend: Text a friend and ask them to give you a number within the chapter's page number range.

- If you are familiar with DBT, you may already know what skills will help you! Refer to the index on page 118 to find the skill you want.

Most of all, repeat after me:

THERE IS NO WRONG WAY TO USE THIS BOOK!

The best, most "right" way to use this book is to use it in a way that will be beneficial to you. You may find yourself always using it the same way, or you may change it up every time. Whatever way works for you works best.

Exploring Materials

Since this is a creative workbook, you have the opportunity to write and make art in its pages. You may want to draw, paint, collage, or journal—so use the space below to test out materials like paint, pens, colored pencils, and glue to see how they look. If a material doesn't work, remember you can always make your art outside of the book.

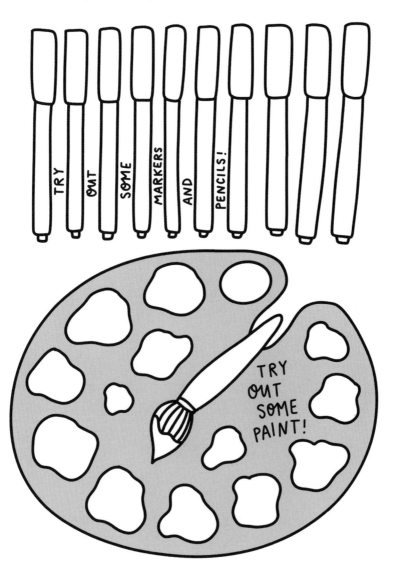

WHAT'S THE FEELING?

Listen, feelings are *hard*. It can be super difficult to parse through all the thoughts and sensations swirling around in our minds and bodies to try and figure out what emotion we're experiencing. Sometimes it's hard because we feel disconnected from our bodies. Sometimes it's hard because the feelings are painful. And sometimes it's hard because we're feeling so many feelings at once—maybe even conflicting ones. We know from the concept of dialectics in DBT that seemingly opposite things can be true . . . so know that you can absolutely be feeling a whole mix of emotions that seem like they can't possibly go together. We are complex! But not to worry—we can use skills like the ones in this section to better identify, understand, sit with, and learn from our emotions and reactions.

There are two different functions for this section. The first is to use the prompts as a tool to determine what emotion you are currently feeling so that you can head to the corresponding emotion section in this book. The second is more of an overarching goal— to use this section to deepen your understanding of emotions and connect with your personal experience of them. So whether you are doing a prompt in this section as a first step or as the only step, you're right where you need to be.

BODY SCAN MEDITATION

Sit comfortably or lie down and let your gaze relax. Take deep breaths and begin by focusing on your toes on one side of your body. Notice how your toes feel. Imagine your breath flowing into them. Repeat the process, moving slowly up your body, from toes to scalp.

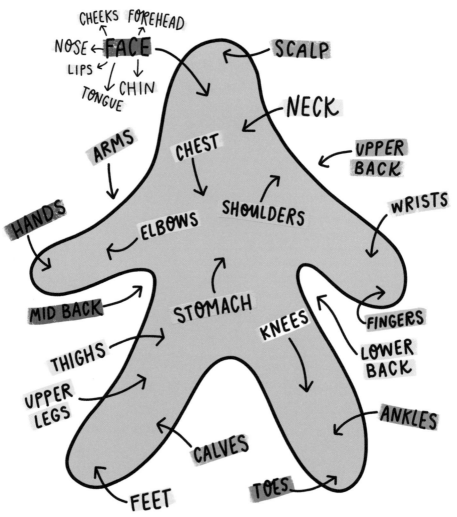

DISTRESS
TOLERANCE

FEELING FLOWERS

Emotions are complex, but we can categorize them into "base emotions." Anger, fear, and sadness are three bases for many of the uncomfortable or difficult emotions. To help identify what you're feeling, fill in the flower petals with some feelings that grow out of each base emotion.

DESCRIBE

Part of the WHAT skills (see pages 114–117)

After we've observed our thoughts and feelings, we can describe them using words and images. Imagine your thoughts and feelings as if they were a book. Name them (title), connect them (add your byline as the author), categorize them (where will these feelings be shelved?). Create the book jacket below, including a front cover and a description of the "book" on the back.

NAME the feeling or thought as the BOOK TITLE!

put IMAGES to the experience—draw or collage!

BY _____

← OWN the experience—put your name as AUTHOR!

 MINDFULNESS

WRITE a description of your THOUGHTS and FEELINGS!

USE your senses and stick to FACTS

LABEL IT!

THOUGHT? FEELING? ACTION?

WRITE any OPINIONS or JUDGMENTS as REVIEWS!

PURPOSE OF EMOTION

You might feel like emotions are pointless—but they actually are very useful and have multiple functions! Let's look at the different purposes of emotions as if they were different parts of a board game.

THINK of YOURSELF AS A **GAME PIECE!**

LIKE DICE, EMOTIONS **MOTIVATE ACTION!**

EMOTIONS are like the other aspects of the GAME.

EMOTIONS **COMMUNICATE** INFORMATION TO OURSELVES!

TITLE DEED EXPRESSION AVE.

EMOTIONS **COMMUNICATE** TO AND **INFLUENCE** OTHERS THROUGH NONVERBAL EXPRESSIONS!

EMOTIONAL REGULATION

EMBRACE CONFUSION

In order to think dialectically, we need to learn to look at all possibilities from multiple sides. One way to do that is by *embracing confusion*—lean into the paradox of opposites and nuances, and be curious. Practice this below by embracing confusion in the maze, and explore *all* the possible ways through it.

YOU MADE IT THROUGH!

OBSERVE

Part of the WHAT skills (see pages 114–117)

We use mindfulness to connect with our emotions. The notes posted below tell us different ways we can observe our feelings. Read each note and try it out.

MEDITATION

Open your mind: Close your eyes, relax, and pay attention to whatever comes up for you.

WRITE OR DRAW WHAT CAME TO MIND

CREATE A CHARACTER
→anger edition←

To create a character card for anger, draw what anger looks like for you and identify its traits and characteristics.

ANGER

♡ ART THERAPY

ANGER

DESCRIPTION

TRAITS

STRENGTHS

WEAKNESSES

LIKES

DISLIKES

CREATE A CHARACTER
↬ fear edition ↫

To create a character card for fear, draw what fear looks like for you and identify its traits and characteristics.

FEAR

FEAR

DESCRIPTION

TRAITS

STRENGTHS

WEAKNESSES

LIKES

DISLIKES

CREATE A CHARACTER
→ sadness edition ←

To create a character card for sadness, draw what sadness looks like for you and identify its traits and characteristics.

SADNESS

♡ ART THERAPY

SADNESS

DESCRIPTION

TRAITS

STRENGTHS

WEAKNESSES

LIKES

DISLIKES

MOOD SCALE

Understanding your mood can help you better understand yourself. Let's make a "scrapbook" to get an overview of your common moods. Use the snapshot templates below to visualize, name, and describe your moods. Remember to include a range of ups, downs, and neutrals!

TIPS! Use familiar language for the mood name (interjections like "meh" are allowed!) ♦ The "photo" can be anything—emoji, color, facial expression, symbol! ♦ Think about how that mood feels and how you identify it. ♦ You can even number them!

♡ ART THERAPY

CLARIFYING GOALS

Not every interpersonal interaction has the same goal. In order to be effective, it is important to clearly identify the goal so we can know how to proceed! Use this page to identify your goal, and then use the *next* page to prioritize.

CLARIFYING PRIORITIES

Our priorities for a conversation depend on our goals for the interaction. Take a look at the doors below to determine what your priorities are for the conversation. Then decorate and number the welcome mats to identify the order of your priorities.

INTERPERSONAL EFFECTIVENESS

COMMUNICATING UNCERTAINTY

Sometimes we want or need support, or want to let someone know how we're feeling, but we don't know what to say because we're uncertain about what we want, need, or feel! Here are ideas for what you could say and space to express your own!

FIGURE OUT FEELINGS

Use this process to sort through a current or recent emotion in order to understand the different components of emotional regulation and see the full picture.

1 CHECK-IN WITH YOURSELF

when our needs aren't met, we can be more VULNERABLE to intense emotional reactions and have difficulty regulating

↳ SEE THE "PLEASE" SKILL (p.106)

↳ NOW PROCEED ↲

2 EVENT THAT ✦ SPARKED ✦ EMOTION

WHAT HAPPENED? STICK TO THE FACTS!

3 THE LENS YOU VIEWED IT THROUGH

INTERPRETATIONS   ASSUMPTIONS
BELIEFS
THOUGHTS   JUDGMENTS

EMOTIONAL REGULATION

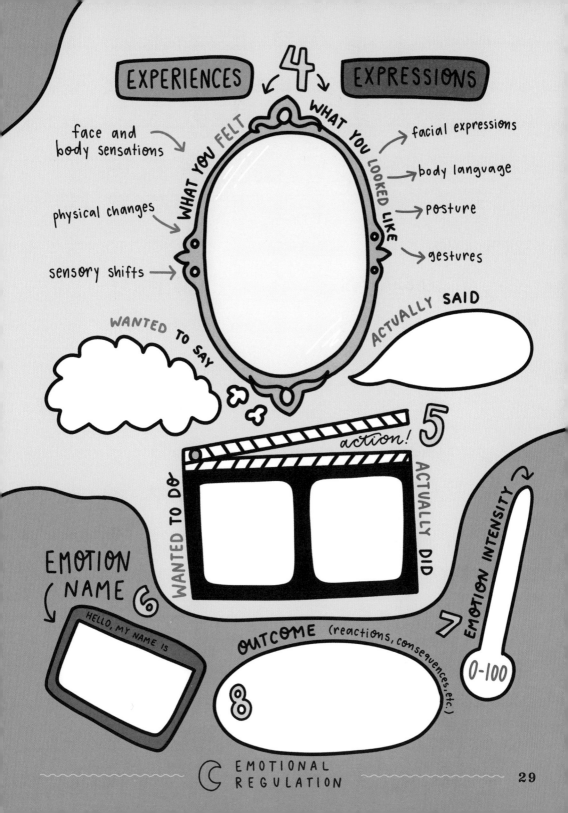

EXPERIENCES → 4 ↓ EXPRESSIONS

face and body sensations →

WHAT YOU FELT

WHAT YOU LOOKED LIKE

→ facial expressions
→ body language
→ posture
→ gestures

physical changes →

sensory shifts →

WANTED TO SAY

ACTUALLY SAID

action! 5

WANTED TO DO

ACTUALLY DID

EMOTION NAME 6
HELLO, MY NAME IS

EMOTION INTENSITY
7
0-100

OUTCOME (reactions, consequences, etc.)

8

☾ EMOTIONAL REGULATION

SOMATIC SENSATIONS

Our emotions aren't just abstract and in our head—they are in our whole body! How we feel mentally can affect how we feel physically. Take a look at the list of sensations and emotions below. Draw a line from each sensation to the emotion(s) you associate it with to create a mind-body connection!

⇒ SENSATIONS ⇐

RACING HEART
SLUGGISH
RELAXED
TIRED
BREATHLESS
COLD
NAUSEOUS
WEAK
RESTLESS
TENSE
HEADACHE
WARM
BLUSHING
TINGLY
DIZZY
HEAVY
EMPTY
AWAKE
JITTERY
BUBBLY
HOT

⇒ EMOTIONS ⇐

SADNESS

ANGER

FEAR

JOY

LOVE

SHAME

DISGUST

SURPRISE

EXCITEMENT

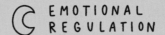

EMOTIONAL
REGULATION

IDENTIFY FEELINGS

Assign a color to each emotion in the key. Think about how each one feels in your body. Use color, lines, shapes, and images on the figure below to show where and how the emotions feel.

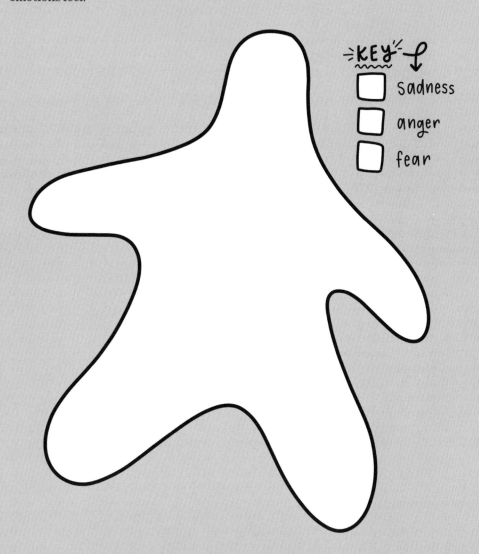

KEY

☐ Sadness

☐ anger

☐ fear

HELLO MY NAME IS

ANGER

Anger is a very misunderstood emotion. Too often it is seen as negative, unhelpful, or even harmful. Anger in and of itself is none of those things—it's what we do with anger and how we behave when angry that has the potential to be those things. Anger is valuable to us when we are able to embrace it and express it. It makes us more creative and optimistic, helps us identify boundaries and values, and motivates us to accomplish things.

There are many different types of anger or emotions that would fall under the anger umbrella. Below are some more specific feeling words that connect back to anger. If you're feeling one of these emotions, or another emotion rooted in anger, then you're in the right spot. The following pages contain skills and activities to help you deal with anger.

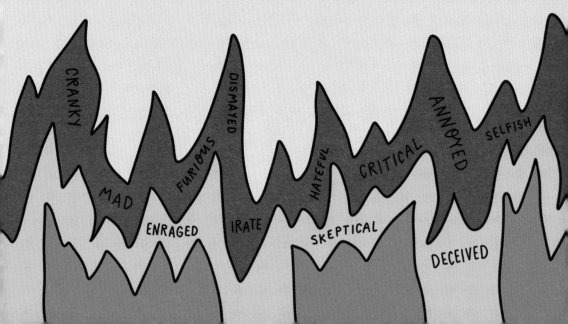

CRANKY

DISMAYED

FURIOUS

MAD

ENRAGED

IRATE

HATEFUL

SKEPTICAL

CRITICAL

ANNOYED

SELFISH

DECEIVED

RANT AWAY

That angry text you want to send? Don't do it. Put it here instead!

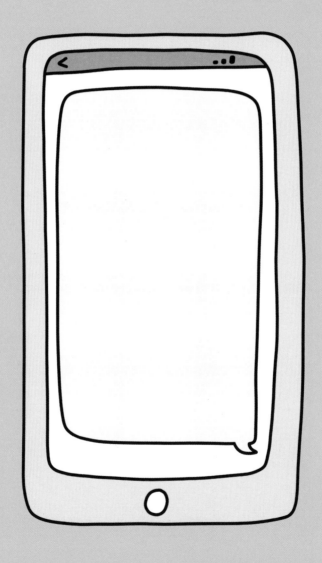

ALTERNATE REBELLION

Sometimes we have the urge to do something destructive or damaging because our emotions are so intense. We can redirect that rebellious urge into something that is still rebellious but not damaging.

COLOR IN THIS **RAINBOW** REBELLIOUSLY

1 Be as MESSY as you want to be—no need to stay in the lines here!

2 Use ANY COLORS you want or have handy, in WHATEVER ORDER feels best to you!

3 Who says it has to be SOLID COLORS? GO WILD with DOODLES and PATTERNS and SCRIBBLES!

MORE *ideas* ON THE BACK! (oh my!)

ALTERNATE REBELLION
→ idea list ←

WEAR YOUR CLOTHES INSIDE OUT!

YELL OR SCREAM!
AAAHHH!

DYE YOUR HAIR!

TURN UP THE VOLUME!
MIN   MAX

WRITE A LETTER
DO NOT SEND
BUT DON'T SEND IT!

WEAR MISMATCHED SOCKS!

SAY NO!
NO.

SLEEP IN LATE!
SNOOZE
12:00 PM

YOU COULD EVEN RIP UP THIS PAGE!

DISTRESS TOLERANCE

SCRIBBLE!

Get that anger out! Scribble furiously.

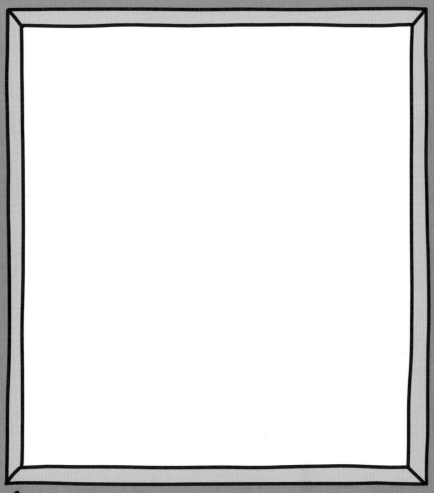

↑Now LOOK at your scribble. Do you SEE anything? Make an IMAGE out of the scribble.

PRAYER

Part of the IMPROVE skill (see pages 114–117)

Prayer means different things to different people—in this instance, it's a phrase or mantra that is directed toward any kind of higher power. It doesn't have to be a traditional or religious idea of higher power—your higher power can be many things. If you're not sure what yours is, take a look at the idea list below. Then, write a prayer that you can say to connect with and open yourself up to your chosen higher power.

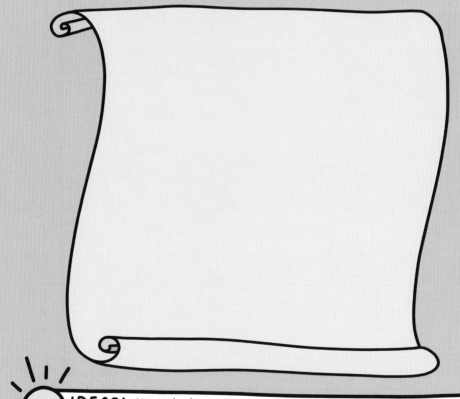

 **IDEAS!** Your higher power could be the universe, the ruling planet of your zodiac sign, God, your wise mind, your higher self, your ancestors, nature, humanity, the sun or moon, the elements, a cultural figure, science... anything you can connect to that is bigger than yourself!

DISTRESS TOLERANCE

DESIGN
your own
prayer
candle

Candles and light are used in many different religious, spiritual, and mindful practices. Use whatever imagery you want to design a prayer candle that goes along with the prayer or mantra you wrote!

INTENSE EXERCISE

Part of the TIP skill (see pages 114–117)

Our emotions can be like a running engine revving us up nonstop. When we feel all amped up from our emotions, engaging in intense exercise can help get some of that energy out, which can make our bodies calmer in the end. Below are some exercise ideas and space to add your own!

LIFT WEIGHTS

ADD YOUR OWN! →

CLIMB UP AND DOWN THE **STAIRS**

GO FOR A **RUN** (or JOG/RUN in place)

LEARN A trending **DANCE**

DO SOME **JUMP** ROPE

DISCLAIMER! Intense exercise may not be suitable for everyone. Listen to your body and consult your doctor, especially if you have health conditions. You can also try the other TIP skills on pp. 46, 60, and 66!

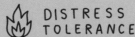 DISTRESS TOLERANCE

MAKE A CHILL PILL

Has anyone ever told you to take a chill pill? Well . . . why not make your own? Fill the pills with ideas to help you relax and chill out (they can be actions or things). Write the instructions for use on the bottle.

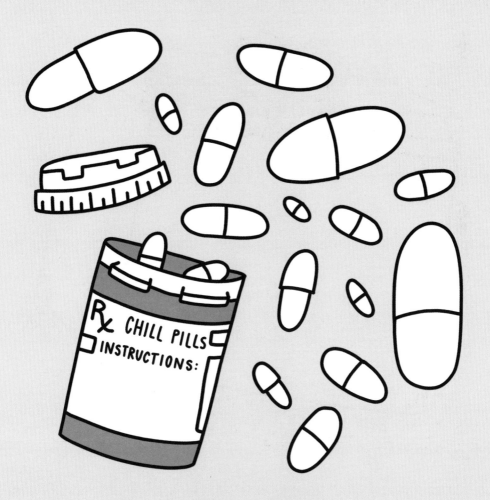

R CHILL PILLS
INSTRUCTIONS:

DISTRACTING with PUSHING AWAY

Part of the ACCEPTS skill (see pages 114–117)

Sometimes our feelings are so intense that we need to push them away for a bit. We're not getting rid of them completely—we're just putting them in a box on a shelf for a little while until we are able to come back to them. Put the feelings that need a pause into the box below and use decorating the box as a distraction.

THE BOX IS LOCKED, BUT DON'T THROW AWAY THE KEY! IT'S IMPORTANT TO REVISIT OUR THOUGHTS AND FEELINGS LATER WHEN WE ARE CALMER AND ABLE TO PROCESS!

 DISTRESS TOLERANCE

ONE-MINDFULLY

Part of the HOW skill (see pages 114–117)

Doing something *one-mindfully* means focusing all of your attention on one task at a time. Practice one-mindfulness while completing the word search filled with joyful words below.

G	S	E	L	K	R	A	P	S	L	R	K	Q	F
L	J	D	C	D	T	P	H	D	W	M	I	B	H
K	N	O	R	G	K	C	S	E	I	P	P	U	P
N	E	L	K	E	N	M	E	W	K	S	I	W	M
K	J	N	K	I	T	I	T	L	L	L	M	B	X
T	E	O	I	M	T	H	C	K	I	O	F	F	O
L	N	W	J	H	E	T	I	N	J	M	V	R	M
A	C	R	X	R	S	A	E	O	A	Z	S	E	A
U	S	I	A	E	C	N	Y	N	N	D	I	S	E
G	U	P	E	P	U	Q	U	Z	S	E	U	H	R
H	Y	F	L	O	W	E	R	S	Q	K	H	A	C
T	D	P	I	H	S	D	N	E	I	R	F	I	E
E	D	X	B	R	E	A	T	H	E	M	G	R	C
R	S	M	R	I	L	X	E	K	O	T	L	K	I

BREATHE   FRESH AIR   JOY   LOVE   SPARKLES

DANCING   FRIENDSHIP   KITTENS   PUPPIES   SUNSHINE

FLOWERS   ICE CREAM   LAUGHTER   SMILE   THERAPY

TURNING THE MIND

Turning the mind means making a commitment to the acceptance of reality. It doesn't mean we agree—it means that we recognize that rejecting reality is causing us suffering and moving toward the path of acceptance will reduce that suffering. Turning the mind is a process we return to regularly in order to keep committing to acceptance.

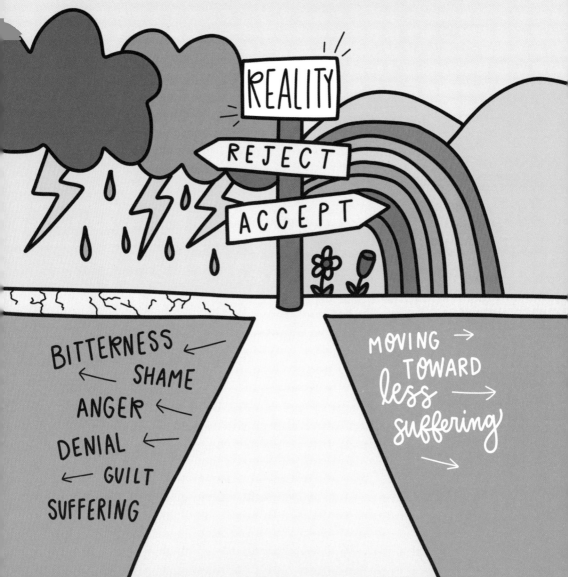

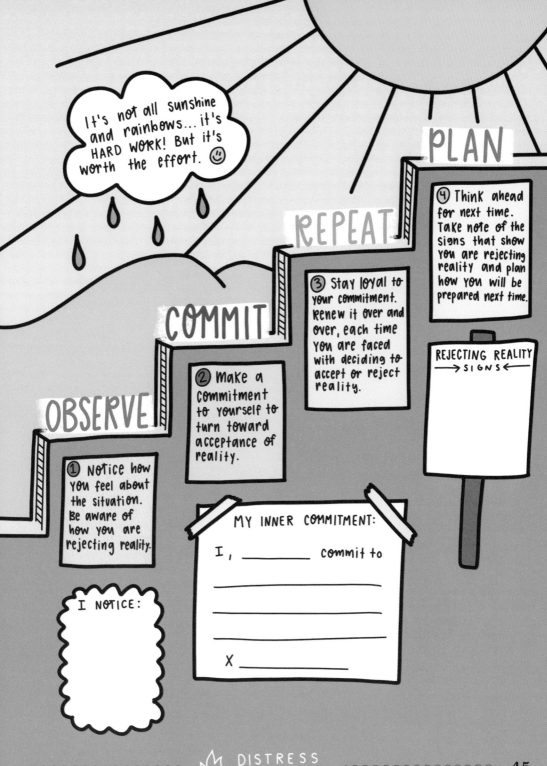

PAIRED MUSCLE RELAXATION

Part of the TIP skill (see pages 114–117)

When we're feeling distress, pairing muscle relaxation with breathing exercises and soothing phrases can help calm our bodies.

BREATHE INTO YOUR BELLY. TENSE ALL YOUR MUSCLES. as you inhale NOTICE THE TENSION. BREATHE OUT, LET GO OF TENSION, and say "RELAX" IN YOUR MIND. FEEL THE DIFFERENCE!

DISTRESS TOLERANCE

RIDE THE WAVE

Emotions come and go, as do the impulsive urges that come with them. The intensity will pass if we wait it out—think of waiting as "riding the wave." Decorate the surfboard to help you pass the time as you ride the wave of your emotions.

STOP SKILL

When we are feeling impulsive or reactive, we can use the "STOP" skill. It helps us pause so we can think before we speak or act, enabling us to move through interactions and situations more mindfully.

1 STOP!
↪ Pause! Don't do anything!

2 TAKE A BREAK
↪ Breathe. Step back for a moment.

3 OBSERVE
↪ Notice how your body and mind feel. Pay attention to your surroundings.

4 PROCEED MINDFULLY
↪ Now that you are more present, continue forward with a WISE MIND (see p. 70)

DISTRESS TOLERANCE

CHECK THE FACTS

Emotions are always valid, but that doesn't mean they always fit the facts of the situation at hand. It can be helpful to take a look at our emotions and consider where they are coming from and whether their intensity fits the situation. Once we check the facts, we can better understand our emotions and determine if we need to problem-solve the situation or change the emotion.

FACT CHECK

www.areyousure.lol

What emotion am I feeling?

What happened to activate the emotion?

What am I assuming/interpreting/thinking about what happened?

DO I FEEL LIKE THERE IS A THREAT?

☐ YES:_____

☐ NO

⌐ NAME IT—A THREAT TO WHAT? CONNECTION, BELONGING, SAFETY?

→ INTENSITY → EMOTION

DO HOW AND WHAT I'M FEELING MATCH THE FACTS?

☐ YES

☐ NO → TIME FOR *OPPOSITE ACTION* (see pp. 88-89)

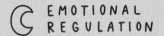

EMOTIONAL REGULATION

PROBLEM-SOLVING

When we are faced with a problem situation, deciding how to proceed can be difficult. Try out this process!

① IDENTIFY YOUR GOAL!

WHAT DO YOU NEED OR WANT?

② BRAINSTORM POSSIBLE SOLUTIONS!

WRITE A BUNCH!

NO JUDGMENTS!

IF YOU'RE COMFORTABLE, TALK THROUGH POSSIBLE IDEAS WITH FRIENDS AND FAMILY!

EMOTIONAL REGULATION

③ Now look at the solutions you came up with and CHOOSE ONE that fits the goal.

TIP!
Try using a pro/con list to choose a solution!
(p.80)

④ GREAT! NOW THAT YOU HAVE YOUR CHOSEN SOLUTION IN HAND, GO TRY IT OUT! THEN, COME BACK TO THIS PAGE! ☺

⑤ EVALUATE

WORKED? yay!

DIDN'T WORK? that's okay!
Look back at your brainstorming list and pick a new solution to try!

HALF-SMILE AND WILLING HANDS

Our body and our brain are *connected*! We can use this connection to calm ourselves, practice acceptance, and even change our emotions.

DISTRESS TOLERANCE

DISTRACTING with EMOTIONS

Part of the ACCEPTS skill (see pages 114–117)

One way to cope with an intense emotion is to distract ourselves by eliciting a *different* one. Think about what might be the opposite of anger—joy? peace? humor?—and use this space to create something that will make you feel that!

IDEAS! Draw something that makes you feel *calm!* Write about a happy or funny memory! Draw or write about a character from your favorite TV show, book, or movie! Make a collage with images of things/people you love!

GIVE

When we have a conversation with someone we care about, especially a difficult conversation, we want to communicate in a way that will preserve the relationship. To do that, keep the GIVE skill in mind during these conversations.

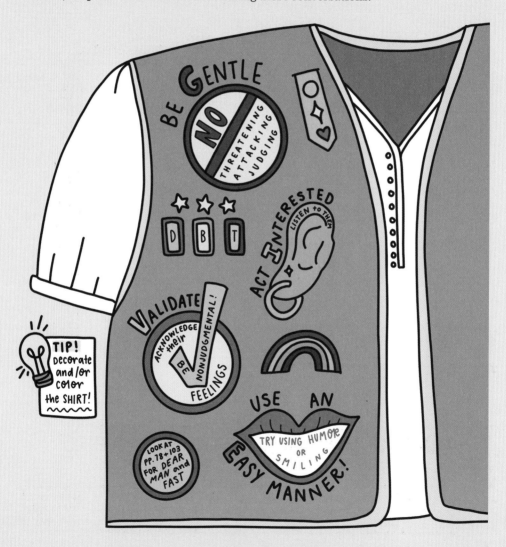

BE **G**ENTLE

NO — THREATENING ATTACKING JUDGING

DBT

ACT **I**NTERESTED — LISTEN to THEM

VALIDATE — ACKNOWLEDGE their FEELINGS, BE NONJUDGMENTAL!

TIP! Decorate and/or color the SHIRT!

LOOK AT PP. 78 + 103 FOR DEAR MAN and FAST

USE AN **E**ASY MANNER! — TRY USING HUMOR OR SMILING

 INTERPERSONAL EFFECTIVENESS

SURROUND YOURSELF WITH GOOD THINGS

Write or draw good things. Note: What constitutes a "good thing" is up to you! There's nothing too small or large.

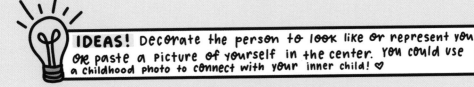

IDEAS! Decorate the person to look like or represent you or paste a picture of yourself in the center. You could use a childhood photo to connect with your inner child! ♡

COMMUNICATING ANGER

Whew! Take a breather. We can feel so much urgency when we are angry and have something to say. If you need to address an incident or situation with someone but are finding yourself feeling too angry to have a productive conversation, try this: First get all the unfiltered thoughts out. Then, take a break and relax. When you're ready, come back to this page and "translate" your angry thoughts into points that are still accurate to your experience *and* will help you communicate more effectively.

let it out...

UNFILTERED!

INTERPERSONAL
EFFECTIVENESS

FOCUS ON FACTS

REFINED!

USE "I" STATEMENTS

BE ASSERTIVE AND STAY ON TOPIC

...then "translate" it.

BREATHE

Fear is one of the most uncomfortable emotions. It is often accompanied by unpleasant physical sensations that may lead to a spiral of discomfort. It's no fun . . . but it is important. Fear has a direct evolutionary purpose, and it's stuck around because it still serves us! Fear is very concerned with all kinds of safety: physical, emotional, mental, spiritual, relational . . . and so on. Our brains constantly scan our environment for threats: from obvious threats to our physical safety to subtle threats to our sense of belonging. Fear is our brains' way of communicating to us that something is wrong.

Now, sometimes our brains can be a little overactive, like a smoke detector that goes off every time you cook. We may get so frustrated by it that we are tempted to just take out the batteries, or so panicked by it that we call 911 and never cook again. Neither of those options is safe or effective, so instead let's recognize that the alarm is trying to keep us safe. Then we can learn what to do when the alarm is blaring.

Fear comes in many forms at varying intensities. Below are some of the different types of fear. If you're experiencing one of these emotions rooted in fear, then you made it to where you need to be: The following pages contain skills and activities to help you work with and around your fear.

• ANXIOUS • REJECTED • THREATENED •
• PERSECUTED •
• EXCLUDED • INSIGNIFICANT • EXPOSED •
• FRIGHTENED •
• CONFUSED •

PACED BREATHING

Part of the TIP skill (see pages 114–117)

TAKE A DEEP BREATH INTO YOUR BELLY

SLOW DOWN THE PACE OF YOUR BREATHING (about 5-6 breaths per minute)

EXHALE LONGER THAN YOU INHALE try inhaling for 4 seconds and exhaling for 7!

DISTRESS TOLERANCE

CREATE YOUR SAFE SPACE

When anxiety and fear make us feel unsafe, it helps to have a safe space to visit in our minds. Use the space below to create yours! You can draw, write, or collage.

THINK ABOUT WHAT HELPS you FEEL CALM AND COMFORTABLE. some ideas to get you started: settings, people, textures, scents, foods, temperature, season, animals, sounds, decorations

CHECK THE FACTS

With no filter, write down the situation that you're reacting to. Then, add check marks next to any notes that are facts and cross out any that are judgments, interpretations, or assumptions.

EMOTIONAL
REGULATION

LOOK FOR:

JUDGMENTS
evaluating or labeling
"should" "good"
"should not" "bad"

EXTREMES
all or nothing thinking
absolutes
"either this OR that"
"never" "always"

OPINIONS
no evidence or proof
"feel" "believe" "think"

INTERPRETATIONS
and
ASSUMPTIONS
meaning we construe or assign
to an experience or situation
often based on past
experiences and fears
"worst-case scenario"

IMAGERY

Part of the IMPROVE skill (see pages 114–117)

Extreme emotions can make it difficult to see anything beyond the current moment.
We can use imagery to imagine other possibilities. Use the crystal ball to envision the
situation you are anxious about. Imagine yourself coping effectively.

DISTRESS
TOLERANCE

GUT FEELINGS

We all get that feeling in the pit of our stomach that we call a gut feeling. Sometimes it can be difficult to determine whether our gut feeling is actually our intuition or if it is fear or anxiety. Use this space to reflect on what your intuition feels like and what fear feels like. What are ways you can tell the difference? In what way(s) do they overlap? Think about physical, mental, emotional, and spiritual cues or sensations.

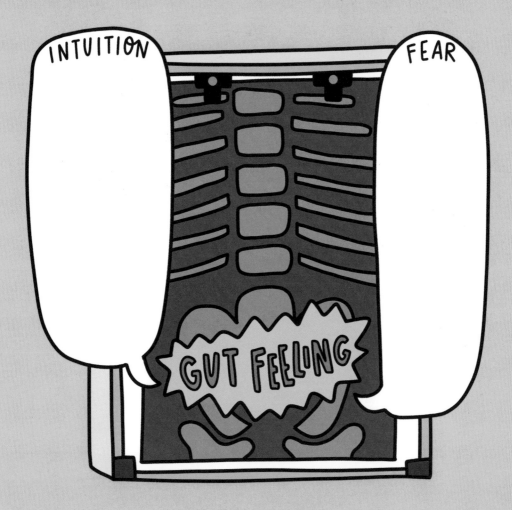

TEMPERATURE

Part of the TIP skill (see pages 114–117)

Cold temperatures are known to help "shock" our system out of an intense emotional experience and can help us calm down. Some ways to try that include:

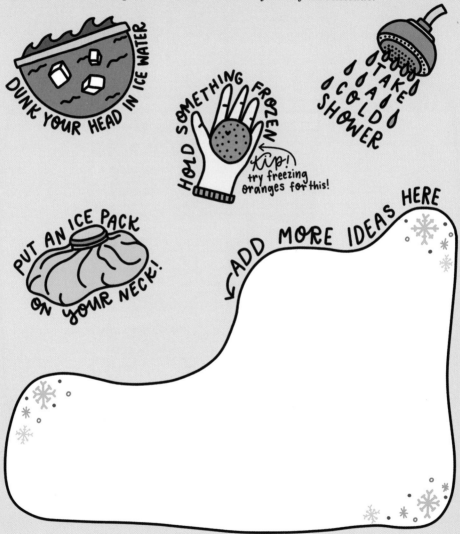

DUNK YOUR HEAD IN ICE WATER

HOLD SOMETHING FROZEN

TIP! try freezing oranges for this!

TAKE A COLD SHOWER

PUT AN ICE PACK ON YOUR NECK!

ADD MORE IDEAS HERE

DISTRESS TOLERANCE

DISTRACTING with ACTIVITIES

Part of the ACCEPTS skill (see pages 114–117)

Make your own BINGO card with activities you can do to distract yourself when you're feeling distressed. They can be calming, fun, physical—you name it! They just need to be things that capture your attention and keep you occupied.

B	I	N	G	O
		✧ "USE ♥ ♥ THIS ✧ BOOK!		

TIP! If you're struggling to think of ideas, check out the bingo card on p.87! Try to include a variety of activities—high energy, low energy, alone, with friends, virtual, at home, out and about!

BUILD MASTERY

Part of the ABC PLEASE skill (see pages 114–117)

We can increase self-esteem and challenge perfectionism through *building mastery*—
or, improving at a skill over time. Choose an activity or skill that isn't too difficult or too
easy for you and use the spaces below to track your progress: Fill in a space each time
you practice. You can color it in, write details of
what you did, or both!

EMOTIONAL
REGULATION

WISE MIND

Wise mind is a core mindfulness skill that helps us find our "inner knowing" that lies in between our other two states of mind: logic and emotion. The ability to find our wise mind by understanding both logic mind and emotion mind helps us make more aligned and effective choices.

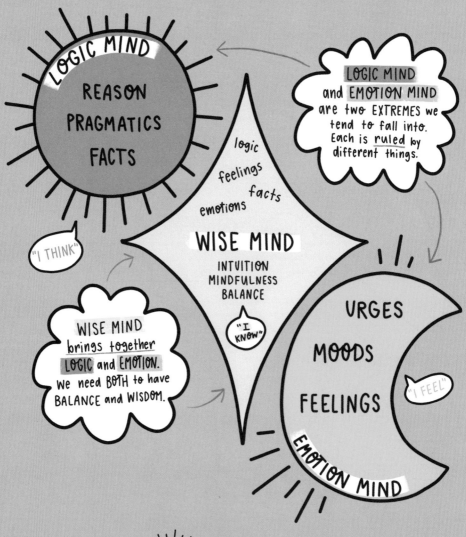

MINDFULNESS

RETHINK THE SITUATION

Sometimes we make assumptions in a situation: We think x = y, and our emotions respond to that scenario and make it hard to see any other possible solution. But it's not usually as simple as x = y; there are often multiple possible explanations! Let's rethink the equation by breaking it down into parts and looking at alternatives..

X = WHAT HAPPENED:

Y = WHAT I ASSUME THAT MEANS:

ALTERNATIVE INTERPRETATIONS:

Y = _____

NOW repeat to yourself this REFRAMED THOUGHT:

"THE FACT THAT _____ HAPPENED DOESN'T MEAN _____"

NONDOMINANT HAND

Use your nondominant hand to draw or write (or both!) in the space below. This practice helps us to challenge perfectionism, embrace uncertainty, and even access our inner child!

♡ ART THERAPY

WALKING THE MIDDLE PATH

We can find our wise mind in any given situation by identifying what each extreme state of mind is saying, and then finding and "walking" the middle path between the two. Try it out below!

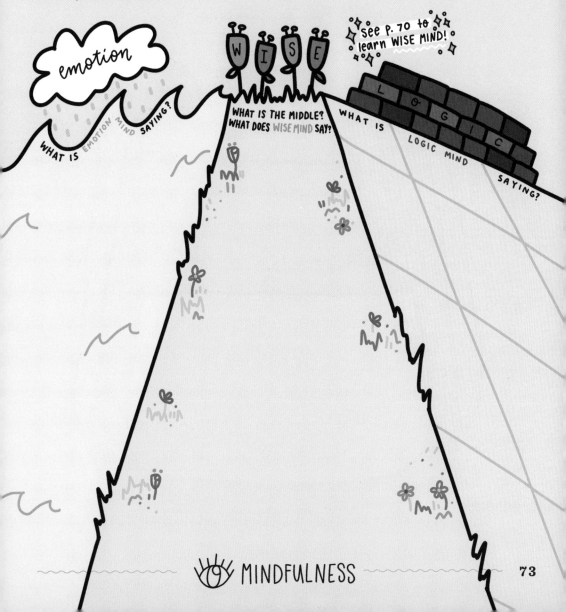

emotion

see p. 70 to learn WISE MIND!

WISE

LOGIC

WHAT IS EMOTION MIND SAYING?

WHAT IS THE MIDDLE? WHAT DOES WISE MIND SAY?

WHAT IS LOGIC MIND SAYING?

MINDFULNESS

COPE AHEAD

Part of the ABC PLEASE skill (see pages 114–117)

We use this technique to plan ahead when we are anticipating a difficult situation or experience. Use this backpack and its contents to describe the situation, list possible challenges in each area, and identify ideas to help cope with each.

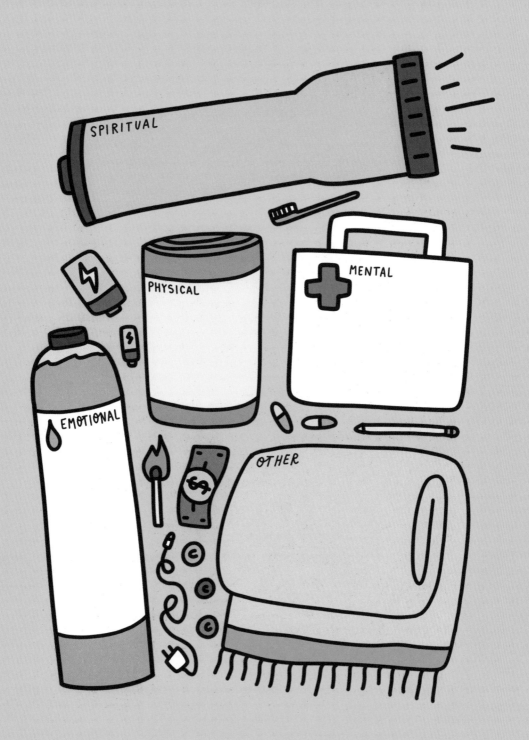

EMOTIONAL
REGULATION

MINDFULNESS MAZE

Mindfulness helps us orient to the current moment. Practice this skill by focusing your attention and bringing your awareness to the present as you find your way through this maze.

FILL THIS PAGE

→ MINDFULNESS MEANS FOCUSING ALL OF OUR *filling this page with it!*

ATTENTION ON ONE THING AND BEING FULLY PRESENT. WE CAN PRACTICE THIS BY CHOOSING A TASK TO DO MINDFULLY. TRY IT OUT BY CHOOSING A COLOR AND

MINDFULNESS
ART THERAPY

DEAR MAN

When there is an objective we need to have met in a conversation (such as setting a boundary, asking for something, or saying no to something), we can use the DEAR MAN skill to increase the effectiveness of the conversation.

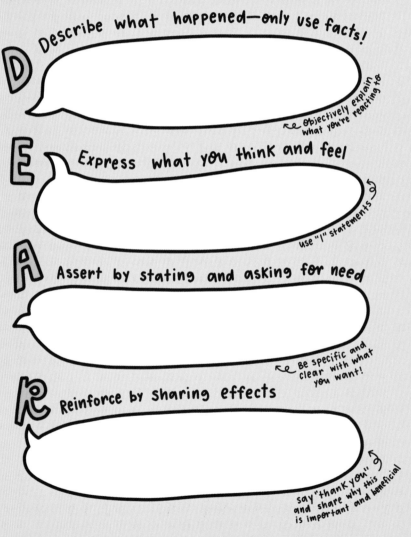

D Describe what happened—only use facts!

Objectively explain what you're reacting to

E Express what you think and feel

use "I" statements

A Assert by stating and asking for need

Be specific and clear with what you want!

R Reinforce by sharing effects

say "thank you" and share why this is important and beneficial

INTERPERSONAL EFFECTIVENESS

During the conversation,

REMEMBER TO:

KEEP "MAN" in mind!

M A N

STAY MINDFUL

→ keep the conversation focused on the topic—no distractions!

→ repeat yourself as needed to come back to the topic.

→ ignore attacks that try to derail or avoid the conversation.

APPEAR CONFIDENT

→ be clear and direct.

→ fake it until you make it... try to look confident even if you don't feel it!

EYE CONTACT

GOOD POSTURE

FIRM BUT SOFT TONE

HOW?

NEGOTIATE

→ be open to compromise

→ ask for their solution

→ know what you're willing to give

"If you ——, I will ——."

PROS & CONS

Making decisions or considering what action to take is hard work—especially if we feel frozen by fear. A pro/con list is something you are likely familiar with . . . but this list has four squares to consider, not just two! Try it out below.

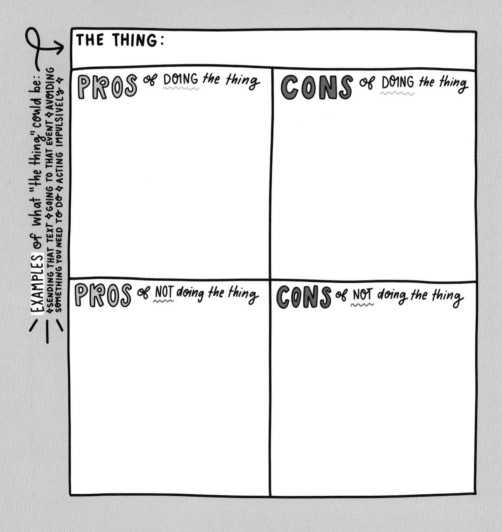

EXAMPLES of what "the thing" could be: ↯SENDING THAT TEXT ↯GOING TO THAT EVENT ↯AVOIDING SOMETHING YOU NEED TO DO↯ ACTING IMPULSIVELY↯

THE THING:

PROS of DOING *the thing*

CONS of DOING *the thing*

PROS of NOT *doing the thing*

CONS of NOT *doing the thing*

DISTRESS TOLERANCE

ASK WISE MIND

We can ask our wise mind for guidance on a situation. Write a question in the speech bubble below. Then use the space in the Magic 8 Ball to sort through your thoughts (logic mind) and feelings (emotion mind).

COMMUNICATION
⤷ FEAR EDITION ⤶

Having anxiety about a conversation you need to have? Fear can make us avoid the things we need to do, like communicate. Use this page to brainstorm and plan out what you want to say!

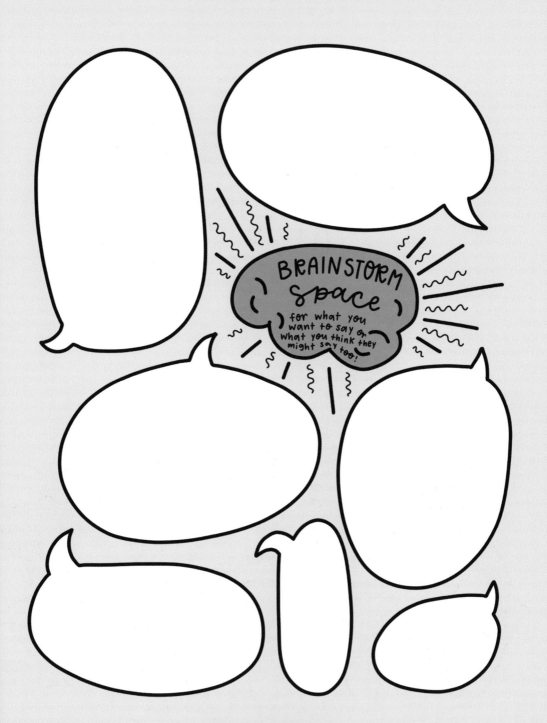

BRAINSTORM *space* for what you want to say or what you think they might say too!

Feeling sad can be such a bummer. It might be cliché, but sadness really is like a heavy cloud looming over us, making things dark and gray and dreary. We may want to cast aside sadness as an unhelpful emotion and make it go away because it's uncomfortable, but there is value in our sadness. It helps us recognize what is important to us, make meaning in our lives, and connect with other people and humanity at large. When we learn how to sit with and feel our sadness, we get to experience the benefits it brings.

There are many different flavors of sadness, and it can be the base of lots of other emotions. Think of sadness as the primary ice cream flavor, and the other, more specific feelings as various flavors made from that base. Below are some of those flavors that connect back to sadness. If you're feeling one of these emotions, or another emotion rooted in sadness, then you're where you are meant to be. The following pages contain skills and activities to help you cope with sadness.

LOVING-KINDNESS MEDITATION

This practice helps us to increase self-compassion and decrease self-judgment. Fill in the phrases on the dandelions below to make your wish. Sit or lie down with your palms facing up and recite the phrases, imagining love and kindness radiating around you. You can also do this meditation to send someone else loving-kindness by inserting their name in the place of "I" in the phrases and envisioning the loving-kindness radiating out of you to them.

~~~~~~~~~ 👁 MINDFULNESS ~~~~~~~~~

ACCUMULATE POSITIVE EMOTIONS
→ SHORT TERM ←

Part of the ABC PLEASE skill (see pages 114–117)

It's helpful to our emotional health to have positive experiences that make us feel good and give us positive memories. We can create short-term positive emotions by doing things that bring us joy, pleasure, and fun! Fill in the BINGO card below with your own ideas, and then start playing!

B	I	N	G	O
TAKE PHOTOS		DO SOMETHING SPONTANEOUS		SING YOUR HEART OUT!
	DANCE		GO ON A ROAD trip	
EAT YOUR FAVORITE FOOD		USE THIS BOOK!		GO THRIFTING
	CREATE SOMETHING		GO OUT WITH FRIENDS	
cuddle or SPEND TIME with ANIMALS		TRY SOMETHING NEW		GO STARGAZING

 TIP! Include a variety of activities: things you can do alone, with friends, for free, at home, outside, when you have low energy (or high!), new things, etc.!

OPPOSITE ACTION

Even though our emotions are valid, they might not always fit the facts of the situation or make sense to act on. Use "Check the Facts" (pages 49 and 63) to figure out whether your emotions fit the situation. If they don't, use *opposite action* to change how you feel. Identify the opposite actions to your feelings, and write them in the space below.

1. WHAT YOU FEEL

2. WHAT YOU WANT TO DO

WHEN I FEEL _____
I WANT TO _____
SO INSTEAD I'LL _____

3. WHAT THE OPPOSITE IS	4. HOW YOU FEEL AFTER DOING OPPOSITE

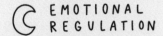

NONJUDGMENTAL STANCE

Part of the WHAT and HOW skills (see pages 114–117)

Oftentimes, we judge ourselves for having an emotion. Our instinct is to try to make it go away as fast as we can. It's important, though, that we let ourselves feel *through* our emotions. One way we can practice this is taking a nonjudgmental stance when observing our emotions. Take a few moments to observe any thoughts and feelings you are having without judgment. Just notice. Then, write what you observed in the magnifying glass below.

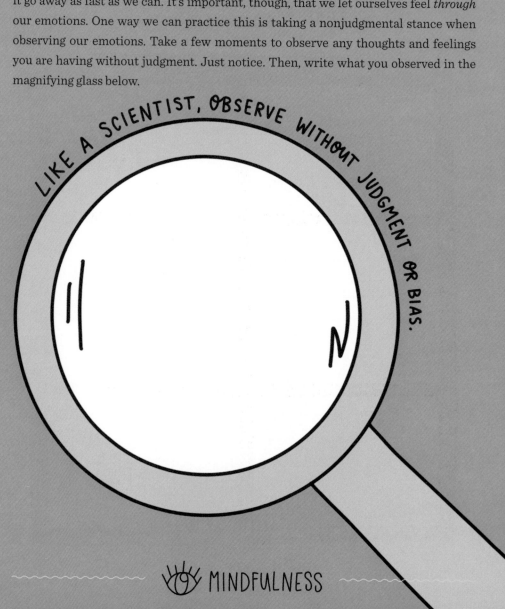

LIKE A SCIENTIST, OBSERVE WITHOUT JUDGMENT OR BIAS.

MINDFULNESS

PERMISSION

Sometimes we hold ourselves to such impossibly high standards that we don't allow ourselves to just be fully messy humans. Fill in this permission slip with the things you grant yourself permission to do.

PERMISSION SLIP

I, _____, grant permission to MYSELF to be HUMAN—including, but NOT LIMITED TO:

☐

☐

☐

☐

☐

☐

FROM NOW UNTIL ETERNITY.

_____
PRINT NAME

_____
DATE

X _____
SIGNATURE

Alyse Ruriani
WITNESS: ALYSE RURIANI
author

THINGS THAT MAKE YOU SMILE

List and/or draw people, places, and things that make you smile or laugh!

♡ ART THERAPY

♡ ART THERAPY

COMMUNICATING SADNESS

Send a picture of this page to a friend or support person when you feel sad to let them know how you feel. Fill it out with your name and pronouns and then circle what you need. You may want to circle with pencil so that you can reuse the page when needed!

HI THERE!

_____ TELLS ME THAT YOU'RE A GOOD SUPPORT PERSON AND ASKED ME TO LET YOU KNOW THAT _____ IS FEELING SAD. IT'S IMPORTANT FOR US TO LET OUR LOVED ONES KNOW HOW WE ARE DOING, BUT THAT CAN BE HARD, SO I VOLUNTEERED TO HELP OUT! THERE ARE LOTS OF WAYS TO SUPPORT PEOPLE WHEN THEY'RE SAD, SO I ASKED _____ TO CIRCLE WHAT ____ WANT(S)/NEED(S)!

time together	cute animal pictures	let me vent	give advice
distract me	validate/ reassure	shoulder to cry on	big hug
play a game together	send memes	⌐ OTHER ¬	

_____   _____   _____

REPLY BACK WITH WHAT YOU CAN OFFER!

♡ THANKS!

HELLO, I AM alyse

↖ HI, I'M THE AUTHOR OF THIS BOOK! I'M A LICENSED PROFESSIONAL COUNSELOR, AN ART THERAPIST, AND AN ILLUSTRATOR!

INTERPERSONAL EFFECTIVENESS

DISTRACTING with EMOTIONS

Part of the ACCEPTS skill (see pages 114–117)

Distracting with emotions means taking an action that elicits an emotion that is different from the one we already feel. Watching a movie or a TV show is one way to make room for a different emotion. You can watch a comedy when you're feeling angry, a thriller when you're feeling sad, or a romantic movie when you're feeling scared. It can be anything, so long as it will bring about a different emotion than the one you're currently feeling. Use the space below to make a reliable list that you can come back to when you need it.

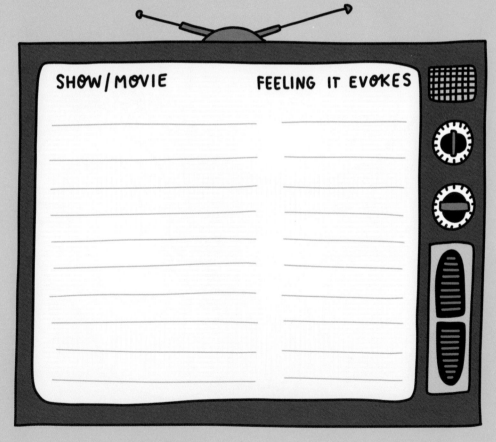

SHOW/MOVIE   FEELING IT EVOKES

SELF-SOOTHE

When we are feeling activated by a strong, uncomfortable emotion, it can be beneficial to reconnect with our bodies. One great way to do this is by using all senses available to us to soothe ourselves. In the illustrations below, list ways you can self-soothe with each sense. Some will overlap, and that's okay, because many experiences have multiple sensations at once!

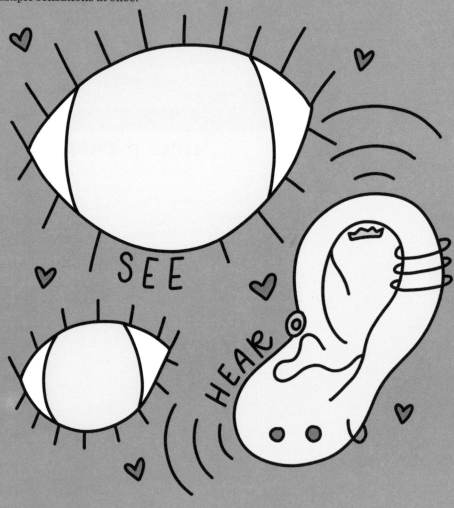

SEE

HEAR

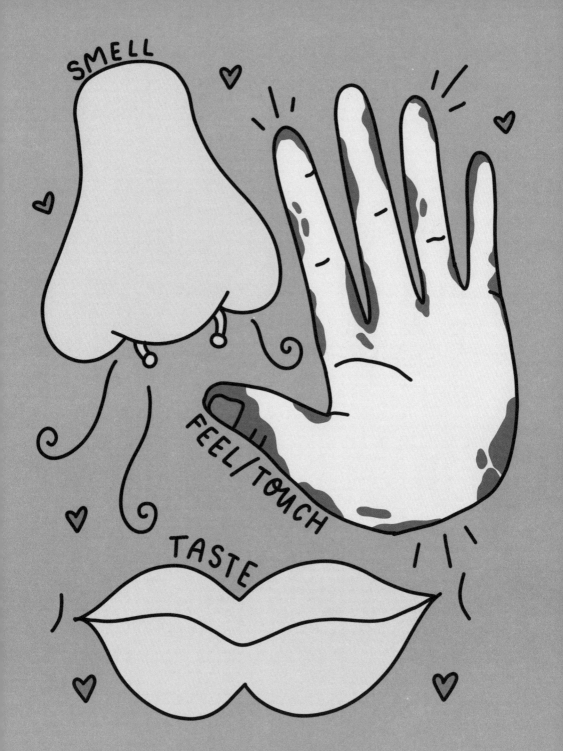

REWARD YOURSELF

Fill out the awards below with accomplishments that make you proud. Nothing is too small—even getting out of bed can be an accomplishment!

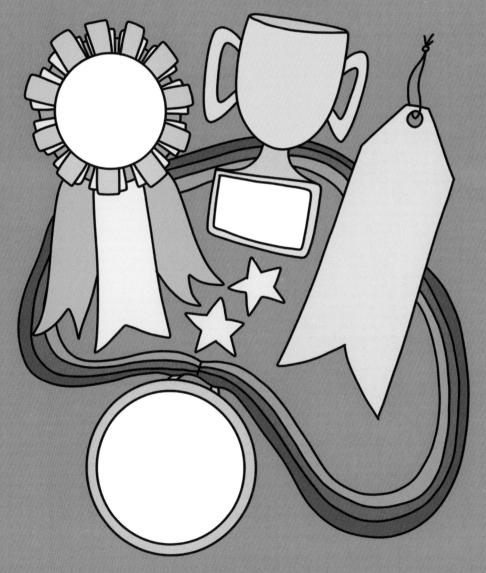

♡ ART THERAPY

SEED PACKET PORTRAIT

NAME AND DRAW YOURSELF AS A PLANT.

THEN IDENTIFY WHAT you NEED TO GROW!

SEED PACKET

INSTRUCTIONS

REQUIRES:

NOURISH WITH:

TIP! Ask yourself what you need, what fulfills you, and what nourishes you. Just as a plant needs water, light, and soil, you have your own needs!

BRIEF VACATION

Part of the IMPROVE skill (see pages 114–117)

Sometimes we just need a vacation . . . and while a real vacation would be fun, most of us can't go on an actual vacation every time we're feeling distressed. But we *can* take a mental vacation! Use your imagination and your creativity to take a brief vacation. Choose where you want to go and fill in the ticket and the snapshot of your destination.

TICKET

THIS IS YOUR TICKET TO *anywhere!* THINK ABOUT WHERE YOU WANT TO GO, AND *fill it in!*

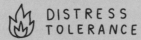

DISTRESS TOLERANCE

now, DRAW, COLLAGE, or WRITE about your trip!

WHAT DOES YOUR VACATION LOOK LIKE?

WHAT WILL YOU DO?

DISTRACTING with CONTRIBUTING

Part of the ACCEPTS skill (see pages 114–117)

We can engage in positive distraction by taking part in something bigger than ourselves and giving back to our communities. Below are some ideas to get you started, along with space to add your own ideas!

VOLUNTEER at an ANIMAL SHELTER

BRING FOOD to a local COMMUNITY FRIDGE

OR GET INVOLVED AT A LOCAL FOOD PANTRY

GIVE SOMEONE A SURPRISE GIFT

PARTICIPATE IN MUTUAL AID

DONATE CLOTHES

OR TAKE PART IN A CLOTHING DRIVE

ADD YOUR OWN IDEAS!

DISTRESS TOLERANCE

FAST

When having a conversation with someone, we want to be sure we are maintaining self-respect. Refer to the FAST skill as a reminder of how to do that.

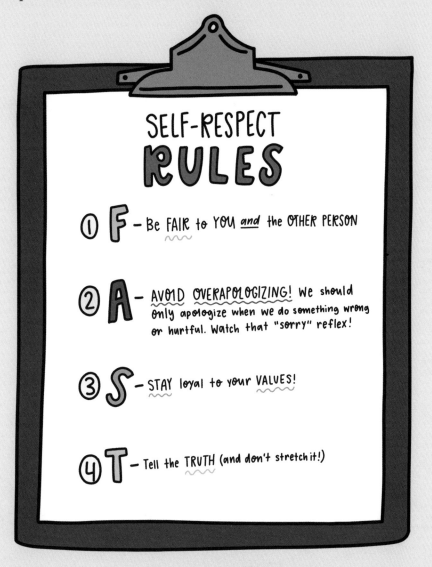

SELF-RESPECT RULES

① **F** – Be FAIR to YOU _and_ the OTHER PERSON

② **A** – AVOID OVERAPOLOGIZING! We should only apologize when we do something wrong or hurtful. Watch that "sorry" reflex!

③ **S** – STAY loyal to your VALUES!

④ **T** – Tell the TRUTH (and don't stretch it!)

ACCUMULATE POSITIVE EMOTIONS
→ LONG-TERM ←

Part of the ABC PLEASE skill (see pages 114–117)

We can each build a life worth living by taking small, value-aligned actions *now* that support our long-term happiness. First, identify five core values from the list below. Choose one to focus on and set goals. Then choose one goal and, in the space provided, name actions you can take to achieve it.

ABUNDANCE	CURIOSITY	HONESTY	PURPOSE
ACCEPTANCE	DEPENDABILITY	HOPE	RECOGNITION
ACCOUNTABILITY	DETERMINATION	HUMILITY	REFLECTION
ACCURACY	DISCIPLINE	IMAGINATION	RESPECT
ACHIEVEMENT	EFFECTIVENESS	INTERDEPENDENCE	SENSITIVITY
ADAPTABILITY	EMPATHY	INTEGRITY	SERVICE
ADVENTURE	EQUITY	JOY	SINCERITY
ALTRUISM	EXPLORATION	JUSTICE	SPIRITUALITY
AUTHENTICITY	EXPRESSIVENESS	KINDNESS	STABILITY
BALANCE	FAME	KNOWLEDGE	STRENGTH
BEAUTY	FAMILY	LEADERSHIP	SUCCESS
BRAVERY	FORTITUDE	LOVE	SUSTAINABILITY
COMFORT	FREEDOM	LOYALTY	TRADITION
COMMITMENT	FRIENDSHIP	MEANING	TRANSPARENCY
COMMUNITY	FUN	OPENNESS	TRUSTWORTHINESS
COMPASSION	GENEROSITY	OPTIMISM	UNIQUENESS
CONFIDENCE	GRATITUDE	ORGANIZATION	UNITY
CONNECTION	GROWTH	PATIENCE	VITALITY
CONSCIOUSNESS	HAPPINESS	PEACE	WISDOM
CREATIVITY	HEALTH	PLAYFULNESS	WONDER

FEEL FREE TO COME UP WITH YOUR OWN!

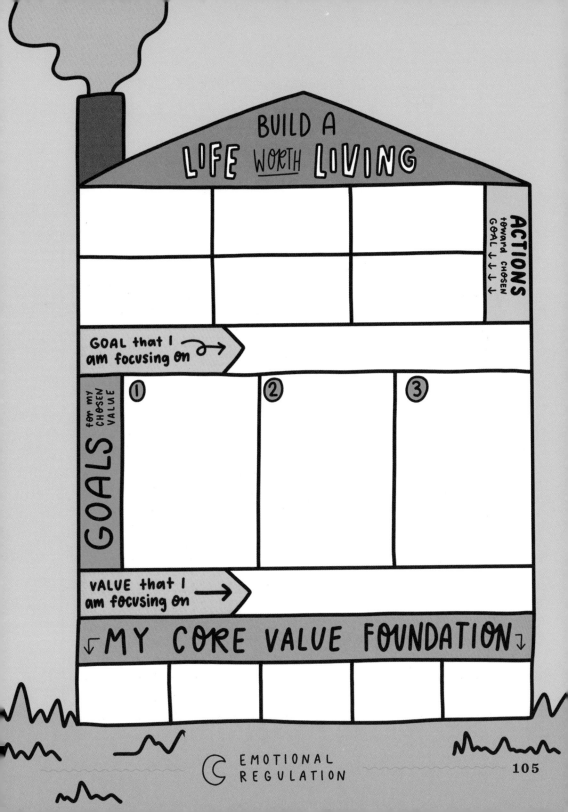

BUILD A
LIFE WORTH LIVING

ACTIONS
toward CHOSEN
GOAL ↓↓↓↓

GOAL that I
am focusing on →

GOALS
for my
CHOSEN
VALUE

① ② ③

VALUE that I
am focusing on →

↓ MY CORE VALUE FOUNDATION ↓

TAKE CARE of YOUR BODY

How we feel physically can impact how we feel mentally (and vice versa). If we aren't taking care of our bodies, it's likely that we don't feel great mentally either. We can increase our ability to emotionally regulate and cope with stressors by taking care of our physical needs. Here is a checklist you can use and personalize!

PHYSICAL SELF-CARE CHECKLIST

	M	T	W	Th	F	Sa	Su
TREATED ANY PHYSICAL ILLNESSES							
TOOK ANY PRESCRIBED MEDICATIONS							
DRANK ENOUGH WATER							
NOURISHED MY BODY WITH FOOD							
WAS MINDFUL of PSYCHOACTIVE SUBSTANCE USE (This includes things like CAFFEINE, ALCOHOL, NICOTINE, AND DRUGS. These things can impact our MENTAL HEALTH, so it's important to be mindful of our usage and be aware of how it impacts us!)							
GOT ENOUGH REST AND SLEEP							
MOVED MY BODY							

Put a mark in the box for each day you complete an activity!

ADD YOUR OWN!

EMOTIONAL REGULATION

COMPLIMENT SHOWER

Go ahead, be vain. Shower yourself in compliments and hype yourself up. You deserve it!

REASONS TO STAY ALIVE

Sometimes, when we feel really, deeply sad, it can feel like the pain is too much. We might even question if it is worth staying alive. Write, draw, or paste in photos of *everything* and *anything*, no matter how seemingly small, that is a reason to stay! You can look back at it whenever you need—and there are crisis resources on pages 112–113, too.

LETTER FROM FUTURE YOU

Write a letter from your future self to you now. What do they want you to know? What words of wisdom, encouragement, or comfort do they have for you?

___/___/___

Dear   ,

Love,

♡ ART THERAPY

ENCOURAGEMENT

color in this page!

I WILL make it THROUGH this!

DISTRESS TOLERANCE

RESOURCES

Just as this book can be a resource for you, there are lots of resources out there to help take care of your mental health. I've compiled some that you can explore as needed. Refer back to this list when you are looking for some additional support!

DBT:

Groups and Therapy
Use an online search engine to look for a local DBT program, DBT skills group, and/or individual DBT therapist.

DBT Self-Help
dbtselfhelp.com

Art Therapy:

American Art Therapy Association
arttherapy.org

Art Therapy Credentials Board: Find an Art Therapist
atcb.org/find-a-credentialed-art-therapist

Finding a Therapist:

therapyden.com
inclusivetherapists.com
goodtherapy.org
openpathcollective.org (sliding scale)
psychologytoday.com

LGBTQIA+ Mental Health:

The Trevor Project
trevorproject.org
Call 866-488-7386
Text START to 678-678

Trans Lifeline
translifeline.org
Call 877-565-8860

National Queer and Trans Therapists of Color Network (NQTTCN)
nqttcn.com

LGBT National Help Center
lgbthotline.org

Black, Indigenous, and People of Color Mental Health:

BlackLine Crisis Line
callblackline.com
Call or text 800-604-5841

The Loveland Foundation
thelovelandfoundation.org

Therapy for Black Girls
therapyforblackgirls.com

Black Mental Health Alliance
blackmentalhealth.com

Sad Girls Club*
sadgirlsclub.org

Asian Mental Health Collective*
asianmhc.org

South Asian Mental Health Initiative & Network*
samhin.org

South Asian Therapists
southasiantherapists.org

Nalgona Positivity Pride
nalgonapositivitypride.com

One Sky Center: The American Indian/ Alaska Native National Resource Center for Health, Education, and Research
oneskycenter.org

StongHearts Native Helpline for Domestic and Sexual Violence
strongheartshelpline.org
Call 844-7NATIVE (844-762-8483)

Therapy for Latinx
therapyforlatinx.com

General Organizations:

Project LETS*
projectlets.org

Fireweed Collective*
fireweedcollective.org

National Alliance on Mental Illness (NAMI)*
nami.org

Mental Health America (MHA)*
mhanational.org

Depression and Bipolar Support Alliance (DBSA)*
dbsalliance.org

American Foundation for Suicide Prevention (AFSP)*
afsp.org

American Association of Suicidology (AAS)
suicidology.org

Peer Support:

* See the organizations listed above that have an asterisk next to them—those organizations have peer support offerings. Some have support groups, some have 1:1 peer support, and some have online peer support spaces.

Warmlines
warmline.org

24/7 Crisis Support:

Suicide and Crisis Lifeline
Call or text 988
Chat online at 988lifeline.org

Crisis Text Line
Text START to 741-741

Living Room Programs
Living Room programs offer an alternative to the emergency room for folks experiencing a mental health crisis. You can use an online search engine to see if there is one located near you.

Peer Respites
Peer Respites are voluntary, short-term, overnight programs that provide community based, non-clinical crisis support run by peers. You can see if there is one located near you on the directories below.

power2u.org/directory-of-peer-respites
peerrespite.com

DBT SKILL SETS

Some skills in dialectical behavior therapy are actually many skills in one. Sometimes they are acronyms (where each letter of the word stands for a subskill) and sometimes they are just a word that houses skills that go together. This glossary compiles those group skills that are sprinkled throughout the book to give a little more context and information. They are organized here by module.

Mindfulness

Note: The WHAT and HOW skills are a group of skills that are intended to be used together. We practice them one by one to learn them, but the goal is to integrate them—giving us the "what" and "how" to be mindful!

WHAT: what to do in order to be mindful

- **Observe** (pages 16, 90)

  Being aware of our internal experience and external surroundings through noticing—not using words

- **Describe** (pages 12–13)

  Putting words to what we have observed; describing it using facts

- **Participate**

  Participating in the moment with full presence and using the other WHAT skills while doing so

HOW: how we do the "what" skills and engage in mindfulness

- **One-mindfully** (page 43)

  Only doing one thing at a time with our full attention and presence. Choosing to focus on the current activity and letting go of other tasks or thoughts.

- **Nonjudgmentally** (page 90)

  Not putting any judgments, opinions, or assumptions on the moment. Staying objective and sticking to facts only.

- **Effectively**

  Putting all the skills together is how we effectively engage in mindfulness!

Distress Tolerance

ACCEPTS: to temporarily distract yourself when experiencing distress that interferes with your ability to effectively engage with the emotion or situation

- **Activities** (page 67)

  Doing an activity that provides distraction and is enjoyable

- **Contribute** (page 102)

  Distracting from the current situation by doing something positive for someone else or the community

- **Comparison**

  Looking at a time where things were worse for us than the current moment and reflecting on how we got through those times

- **Emotions** (pages 53, 95)

  Eliciting a different emotion through an activity to distract from the current emotion

- **Push Away** (page 42)

  Separating yourself from the current situation and emotions by pushing them away for the time being, until the distress has lowered and you are able to come back to it.

- **Thoughts**

  Getting your mind to think about something else

- **Sensations** (pages 96–97)

  Using your five senses to ground yourself and calm your nervous system

TIP: biology-based skills to physically calm down your body

- **Temperature** (page 66)

  Using cold temperatures to "shock" the system and activate your parasympathetic nervous system, which increases relaxation and decreases stress

- **Intense Exercise** (page 40)

  Releasing pent-up energy through movement

- **Paced Breathing** (page 60)

  Intentional, slow breathing to relax the body and promote mindfulness

- **Paired Muscle Relaxation** (page 46)

  Releasing tension in your body through tensing and releasing muscles

IMPROVE: to get through a difficult situation and "improve" the current moment

- **Imagery** (page 65)

  Using imagination and visualization to transport ourselves mentally

- **Meaning**

  This one is not in this workbook but is a skill that involves finding or creating meaning from difficult experiences

- **Prayer** (pages 38–39)

  Looking to and connecting with something bigger than ourselves to gather strength

- **Relaxation**

  Engaging in activities that calm our bodies and minds. (This one isn't listed by name in this workbook, but many of the prompts that use our senses could also be considered this skill!)

- **One Thing in the Moment**

  This one isn't labeled in the book but overlaps with many of the mindfulness skills! It's similar to "one-mindfully" in the mindfulness section, but is more specifically about bringing our attention to the current thing we are doing in this moment.

- **Vacation** (pages 100–101)

  We all need to take a break sometimes. While vacations are awesome, this skill isn't actually about taking a real vacation. It's about taking a "brief vacation" from daily life for a few hours or a day in order to give yourself a break. Sometimes we do this by visualizing a vacation and sometimes we do this by doing a relaxing, pleasurable, or leisurely activity.

- **Encouragement** (page 111)

  Giving yourself some encouraging words through affirmations and self-compassion.

Emotional Regulation

ABC PLEASE: to increase resiliency and decrease our vulnerability to emotion mind

- **Accumulate Positive Emotions**

  We can increase the amount of positive emotions by increasing our positive experiences! Having experiences that feel good improves our mood and our ability to tolerate the bad times, too. When accumulating positive emotions, we want to look at both short-term and long-term experiences.

- **Short Term** (page 87)

  Experiences we engage in regularly that accumulate positive emotions in our day-to-day life

- **Long Term** (pages 104–105)

  Steps we take to create lasting experiences that align with our values and bring meaning to our lives

- **Build Mastery** (pages 68–69)

  Learning and improving at something increases our self-esteem and confidence. We can incorporate this into our lives by practicing and increasing our skill level in a hobby or activity.

- **Cope Ahead** (pages 74–75)

  Sometimes we know a difficult or stressful experience is coming up. Preparing and making a plan for how we will cope keeps us from having to figure it out once we're in the thick of it.

- **PLEASE** (page 106)

  This is a reminder to take care of our bodies through attending to our health and our needs. This means treating any illnesses, nourishing our bodies with food and movement, getting enough sleep, and being aware of how mind-altering substances affect our well-being.

Interpersonal Effectiveness

Note: I didn't split these skill sets up in the book, but am including them here since they are also acronyms that combine a set of skills! Turn to the page listed for explanations.

- **DEAR MAN:** communicate wants and needs effectively (pages 78–79)

  Describe, **E**xpress, **A**ssert, **R**einforce
  Mindful, **A**ppear confident, **N**egotiate

- **GIVE:** maintain healthy relationships when communicating (page 54)

  (be) Gentle: No attacking

  (act) Interested

  Validate

  (have an) Easy Manner

- **FAST:** keep your self-respect during communication (page 103)

  (be) Fair

  Avoid Overapologizing

  Stick to values

  (be) Truthful

INDEX

ACKNOWLEDGMENTS

It feels unreal to be writing acknowledgments for an actual published book that I created. There are so many people I want to thank who made this book possible. First I want to thank my team at Workman, who brought this book to life. Sarah Curley, Anna Cooperburg, and Megan Nicolay—thank you for your vision and support of my work. It was an honor to have not one but three amazing editors being part of this at different stages. To everyone at Workman who contributed to this workbook, especially my designer Sarah Smith: Thank you, thank you, thank you.

Next, I would like to thank my family—especially my mom, Deborah, my dad, Ross, and my sister, Brynn (aka sisterdoodle)—for your love, guidance, and celebration of my achievements. You all know what it took to get me here and I'm so grateful for each of you.

A huge thank you to my best friend, Ellen Oanes. Thank you for proving that healing happens in relationships, for being there for the ups and downs, and for being the Cristina to my Meredith. Thank you to both you and Jonathan for the hot meals, surprisingly comfortable camping mattress, and kitchen table where a lot of this book came to fruition.

To all of my friends who hold many roles—cheerleaders, advice-givers, meme-senders, thought-provokers, collaborators: my fieldwork babes (Jacqueline, Gina, Gia, and Candice), my college friends (especially Tess, Alex, Erica, and Devon), my divas in diapers (Kathleen and Nicole), my art therapy pals and all of the loved ones in my life who have supported me in various ways —thank you. I wish I could name you all, but what a gift that there wouldn't even be enough space to do so. I am so grateful for the community I have around me.

To my past and present mentors who've helped me be who I am today, thank you for sharing your knowledge with me, challenging me, and helping me cultivate my skills and talents. I'd especially like to thank Katharine Houpt, my art therapy comics professor—I started drawing because of your class. Thank you for showing me that I can, in fact, draw.

To my therapist, Emily: Thank you for helping me create connections I struggled to find on my own and for providing a safe place for all parts of me. To all of my past therapists that helped me get to where I am today—either by showing me the healing that therapy can provide or for inspiring me to be the therapist I needed them to be—thank you.

To my clients, the wonderful people I have or had the honor to work with: Thank you for letting me into your inner world. It is an honor to sit with you in the messiness of life, and I'm grateful for all that I learn from our work together.

To my cat Boo, thank you for being cute and cuddly. I know you're glad this book is finished since it took up so much of my time and now my hands will be free to hold you more. You're a fantastic emotional support animal and co-therapist.

And finally, to myself—especially my younger selves: Thank you for getting me here through all the twists and turns. I know it wasn't always easy, and it didn't always feel worth it, but damn, am I proud of us. I hope you can be too. You did it.

ABOUT THE AUTHOR

ALYSE RURIANI (she/they) is a queer femme art therapist, licensed professional counselor, illustrator, and person with lived experience. She holds a Bachelor of Fine Arts in Graphic Design and a Masters in Art Therapy and Counseling. Alyse's work aims to communicate information, provide tangible tools, and validate the human experience through engaging illustrations and designs. They live in a colorful apartment in Chicago with their black cat/co-therapist Boo. When Alyse is not working, you can likely find her swimming in some body of water, making art with friends, or hyperfixating on some new idea.

You can find Alyse in various corners of the internet:

@ALYSERURIANI
INSTAGRAM / TIKTOK / TWITTER

www. alyseruriani .com
WEBSITE & ONLINE SHOP